I GAVE IT TO THE PAGES

ZEMI HOLLAND

Nassau, Bahamas

I Gave It to the Pages
All Rights Reserved
Copyright © 2014 by Zemi Holland

All rights reserved. No part of this publication may be reproduced, stored in a retrieval system or transmitted, in any form or by any means, without prior written permission of the publisher, nor be otherwise circulated in any form of binding or cover other than that in which it is published and without a similar condition being imposed on the subsequent purchaser.

ISBN-13: 978-1495302886
ISBN-10: 1495302881

Cover Design: Christina Darville

Published by Zemi Holland
Nassau, Bahamas

Printed in the United States of America

In Memory of Deanna

Dedicated to every woman trying to live beautifully.

May this book encourage you to turn your pain into art.

ZRH

CONTENTS

Spoken Through the Wire   1
L[i/o]ve   2
A Love Letter to the Soul   3
My Lips   5
His Mama Said   6
Art   8
Butterfly Rising   9
Pain and Purpose   10
Deficiency   11
Protected   12
Bye, Bye Fluttering Angel   13
Deanna   14
Donovan Died   19
Wounds   20
Good Morning   21
The Lies   22
Modern Day Pauper   23
Tears Dry   24
Apples & Trees   25
In Misery I Am Yours and You Are Mine   26
My Little Lie   28
Psalm 51   29
Girl on the Bus   30
The Thin Line   31
I Am Dust   32
Taken   34
Black Bird Pie   35
His Girl   36
Running On and Out of Love   37
Expectations   38
Hang Me Up One Time   39
My Heart   40
Ladies, Stop Kissing Frogs   41

Used To 42
Fantasy/Fallacy 43
RunDriveSwim Cowards 44
Wilting Flower 45
It's Okay 46
The Ex 50
Smoke & Ashes 51
Overstanding 52
Diary of A Teenager – Part I 53
Strange Snowmen 56
Vain Attempts 58
Yup, I'm a Woman 59
Big Belly Girl 60
Wise Men Are Proactive 61
Eleuthera 62
Lukku-Cairi 64
Assurance 66
Nut Shell 67
Cinnamon Scented Day Dream 68
Delonix Regia: The Flame Tree 69
Just a Wish 70
Pillow Talk 71
Family Reunion 72
Please Visit the Garden 73
Spring Time, Growth Time 74
Now 75

FOREWORD
By Wendy Coakley-Thompson

True confession time: I envy poets. I'm jealous of their abilities as word economists to encapsulate in verse what takes novelists like me thousands of words to capture. Their thoughts are no less fecund, their expressions of life's universality no less meaningful. I am in awe of poets in general and of one in particular—Zemi Holland.

Please feel free to assume that I am biased. I am guilty as charged. You see, Zemi Regine—her very name being its own lyrical meter—is flesh of my flesh and blood of my blood. She, like me, is from the long lineage of Coakleys, and Barnetts, and Bethels, and Deans—families with roots that sink deep into Bahamian soil. Zemi is my beautiful cousin whom I've known from afar. As I read *I Gave It to the Pages*, Zemi's collection of deeply personal poems, the 25-year age difference between us becomes a mere blip, and I watch Zemi—the feisty wild child that I'd known mostly in her pupa of girlhood—emerge from her cocoon into a soulful woman and artist. *I Gave it to the Pages* is aptly and appropriately titled.

I Gave it to the Pages is a feast for all. Those who live for poetry will embrace the multitude of emotions that the collection evokes. The ambivalent, who might have read their last poem under extreme duress in school, will find the collection highly accessible. The work itself, with its spare fullness and coy honesty, illustrates that life, like poetry, is an oxymoron. Some of the offerings included in the book are free verse; some rhyme; some read like prose. Fundamentally, though, *I Gave it to the Pages* has something for everyone. The romantic in me responds to the dizzyingly sparse jabs of "L[i / o]ve." Those of us with mother issues will definitely vibe with the *Our Mothers, Ourselves* thread interwoven throughout "Apples and Trees." Some of the poems, like "Art," are light, shy, hesitant cuts that hint at the slashes at the heart to come.

True confession, Part 2: I've cheated. Unlike the uninitiated reader just experiencing Zemi for the first time, I come to her work with knowledge of her backstory. I especially know about the losses that Zemi has suffered throughout her young life. Zemi was a mere child when she witnessed the death of her mother, Deanna. Those of us adults within the family, as we grieved for our precious cousin, could only imagine how such a devastating loss would manifest itself in the lives of her children. The eponymous poem, "Deanna," partially answers our question. More death. Zemi had an older brother, Donovan, who had drowned before Zemi could know him. In the poem "Donovan Died," the twin loss of mother and brother meet at a literary crossroads, as Zemi, it seems, tries to make sense of the senseless. In "Please Visit the Garden," Zemi sweetly calls out for her recently deceased grandmother, Audrey. Zemi has skillfully used poetry as a tool to explore experiences that would have rocked lesser souls.

Even as I project, though, I'm unsure whether or not her words mean what I think they meant to her. Does, for example, "His Mama Said" reflect a longing of a motherless woman for a departing lover? Is "Bye, Bye Fluttering Angel" also about the loss of Donovan? And why is "Psalm 51" so named? Though poignant, it bears absolutely no resemblance to the Psalm 51 in my King James Bible. But art doesn't need to make sense to move you, right?

Some may say that poetry is nothing without the mention of love. Here, Zemi does not disappoint—from the adorable "His Girl." To love gone wrong in the benign sense ("The Thin Line") to the malignant ("Girl on the Bus"). There's also the power of survival post-love or its perversion of it ("Used To", "It's Okay"). I didn't need the Rosetta Stone to follow along with the message here. It was crystal, and at times brutally, clear.

In *I Gave it to the Pages*, I am acutely reminded that my cousin, at heart, is an island gal. Even through her unique name—which means the physical manifestation of a spirit or ancestor in the Arawak language—she embodies our history. She explores this heartbreaking history in "Lukku-Cairi." As a perfect counterweight, she muses, in "Eleuthera," about the idyll that forged her. She also illustrates her gift of empathy in "In Misery I Am Yours and You Are Mine," written in response to the 2010 earthquake in Haiti, the Bahamas's southern neighbor. It is Bahamian custom to bury a baby's umbilical cord in the soil. Such connectedness to the island is a running theme throughout *I Gave it to the Pages*.

As I read and revel in Zemi's work, I am reminded overall that the words on the pages are those of a multi-faceted young artist with such an old soul. I am certain that the universality of the poems in *I Gave it to the Pages* will resonate as much for others as they do for this author knocking on her fifth decade on the planet. Hopefully, Zemi's well-lived life will give birth to more expression through verse. For all the pain, love, and loss that Zemi has experienced has produced a woman with a bottomless gift, of which we are lucky to partake. I am extremely proud to share the gene pool of such a talented force of nature.

I Gave it to the Pages is Zemi Regine Holland's opening salvo. With it, she has dropped the mic and walked away, allowing her words to resound. Just like that—a masterful poet enters our sphere with a big, bad briggadum bam!

Wendy Coakley-Thompson, PhD
Author, *Writing While Black*, *Triptych*, *What You Won't Do For Love*, and *Back to Life*
Herndon, VA

Spoken Through the Wire

All I have left is my artistry
All I can give you is my creativity
All I can send you is my voice
While my heart mends behind the haven of my ribs
And my lungs learn how to fully expand again
One day I'll be able to love again
And I'll hold your hand close to my heart
Like I hold this microphone

L[i/o]ve
Spinning.
Dizzy.
Tumbling.
Hold me up.

This
Love
Thing
Got me all out of my head.

What is up?
What is down?
Where am I?

Sleepless nights.
Silent tears.
Laughter.
The joy.
The pain.

Ouch.

A Love Letter to the Soul

Journey under the epidermal layer of my skin
Take a walk along the membrane of the cells
That make up my body
Swim in the cytoplasm of the inner me
Enter my eyes
Travel along the optic nerve
Welcome to my brain

Observe the fabric of the woman you seek to know
Catch hold of the impulses that run along my spinal cord
Jump into my blood stream and flow into my heart
You're welcome there

Watch as emotions, platelets and blood cells
Flow through the chambers
Pick an emotion to call your own and hold it tight
Draw your name in both my heart's ventricles
Leave your mark there forever
Leave your mark here forever

I'll embrace you with open arms
I'll look deep into your eyes
I shall not be afraid
I shall hold you close
I shall not let go
Even when our arms part
I shall still be holding on

I am not afraid to be broken
Not afraid to cry
Not afraid to open up
Never too scared to try
I shall smile big each time I see you
Shine bright with each spoken word
Laugh internally when I hear you
Blush eternally from your candid heart

I will let all of my emotions out
I will never hide a feeling
I shall treasure you always

In each word
In each touch
In each glance
In each smile
In each embrace
You shall feel my truthfulness

The day a word becomes an action
The day a heart becomes a swinging door
The day a mouth is always sincere
Is when each feeling shall be revealed
For you
To you
Only you

Travel inside of me
Learn my thoughts like the palm of your own hand
Reach the depths of my soul
And leave your mark there
Leave your mark here
Forever

My Lips

pomegranate stained
and mine they
won't be touched
pink from birth
with a line down
the middle of the
bottom from the
hit of a softball
pushed out like the
beak of a duck
pouted to show
dissonance and the
faded memory of
a five year old girl
beautifully shaped
and bowed down
to greet your majesty
saved just for me
no French kiss
to evoke bliss
no slow lingering touch
of pink to brown
they're mine
and with me is
where they belong

His Mama Said

Rolan's mother loves him
She's strong and wise
Gentle, rough and kind
All at the right time
Sometimes I wish someone else's mother was mine

Can we share?

I listen to the words she says
And imagine my mummy would say them too
If she could
He said,
She just gives me love and says that [heartbreak] is normal.

Mummy can you give me love
And make me normal?
I search the world for your words
And respect all mothers (even the bad ones)
Because they all bring messages from you
Their lives show me what to do and what not to do

His mother told him,
God probably has something better for you.
To ease his pain for a love he lost
And he listened
Because that's his Mother

She has years of experience
It shows in the lines of her hands
You see it spread evenly in a nice thin layer
As she spreads the cream
She's wise
And, best of all, she loves him

Don't force anything.
Just keep going through life and be strong.
People come into your life for a season and for a lifetime.
Maybe she was only there for a season.
You should not think that she is the center.
Everyone thinks like that.

Just give it time and you will meet somebody else.

No matter how many times I told him those very words
Nothing hit him harder
Hugged him tighter
Lifted him higher
Or stroked his head more gently
Than the words of his very own
Mother

Art

I love art
You would too
There are lots of things to do

Draw a picture
Sculpt some clay
You can do it all day

Finger painting
Is lots of fun
Pin it up when it's done

c. 1995

Butterfly Rising
(For All Young Women)

Lift up your head
Ain't nothing on the ground but dirt
Forget what they said
No one can tell you what you're worth
You're a piece of the puzzle bigger than the world you see
That's how you fit perfectly next to me
You're gonna
rise
rise
rise
Your soul is a butterfly
Go on and
fly
fly
fly

Pain and Purpose

The sun rises. The sun sets.
Tears fall. Tears dry.
I'm wrapped up in the earth
soaking up your pain.
I'll grow strong
because of misery.
Green. Living. Alive.

Deficiency

Silver linings
grace white clouds.
Give me one
please.

Protected

Count my ribs and know
the number of bars
that protect my heart.
Count my scars and see
how many times
they tried to get in.

Bye, Bye Fluttering Angel

The only one I was ever afraid to lose flew away.
Did you see that butterfly fly away?
He was such a beautiful angel.
Cry on the wings of a firefly.
Cry on the wings of a dragonfly.
But you can never draw pretty pictures
Like those on the wings of a
Butterfly.

Deanna

Dark night.
Death is lurking.
Death is hiding.
Disguise.
Demise.
Deceit.

Knocks at the door.
Asthma's here.
Constricting.
Clogging.
Stopping.
Killing.

She can't breathe.

Wrong medicine.
Wrong doctor.
Wrong night.
Wrong age.
Wrong person.
Wrong mother.

Wrong.

Early morning.
I hold her hand.
"Lord, help me!"
She can't take the pain.
She's hurting.
Should I let her go?
Don't make me choose.
I want her here.
More begging.
She and I.
She wins.
He wins.

Unconsciousness.

Wake up.
Don't go.
Stay Mummy!

Shani, Zane, Zemi:
Crying.
Sobbing.
Wishing.
Hoping.
Praying.
Please?

No.

She couldn't take it.
She's worked too hard.
Worked too long.
She's tired.

Nurse Holland's gone.

"No more mummy baby, no more."
That's what they told me.
That's what killed me.
Killed me.
Killed her.

She's dead.

Lifeless.
Smiling.
Free.
Without me.
Sky blue.
Heart dark.

Silence.

Donovan,
Lead her home.
To her father.
To mama and papa.
To you...her son.

Left to mourn?
The kids.
The husband.
The mother.
The brothers.
The family.
The friends.
The patients.
The neighborhood.

She was loved.

Late afternoon.
Walking weeping willows.
Handkerchiefs trailing behind.
Onward to the church.
Onward to the graveyard.

Stop.

Tomb stones.
Black.
White.
All black.
Tissue.
Tears.

Pain.

Empty hole.
Inside?
Her coffin.
Her body.
My heart.
Gone forever.

Gone.
Forever.

Couldn't touch her.
Couldn't see her.
Wanted?
Her laugh.
Soft touch.
Soft curls.
Her hugs.
Her love.

Lost.

Tears burn.
Eyes red.
Heart aching.
No eating.
Thin.
Thin.
Thin.
Sleeping?
I can't remember.

I died with her.

Flowers.
Food.
People.
Doors open.
Doors close.
Night.
Day.
What's the difference?
Last week I had a mother.
Last year she was here.
Today?

Nothing.

Early evening.
At the beach.
Floating in salinity.
Staring up at the sky.

Thinking.

She was my favorite.
Sorry Daddy.

Shooting stars
Pierce my heart.
No hope.
Fragments of a wounded being.
Find me in the cracks of life.
I'm buried in her coffin.
I'm etched into her bones.
I'm dead...even today.

Seconds.
Minutes.
Hours.
Days.
Weeks.
Months.
Years.

All have passed without her.

Today.
Yesterday.
Forever.
I want no one.
I want no thing.
I want nothing.
Only her.

Only Deanna.

Donovan Died

Mummy I know you cried for him.
I know you cried for him.
I know you cried for him.

Now we cry for you.
We cry for you.
We cry for you.

But you're with him.
You're with him.
You're with him.

So you can stop crying
And one day we'll stop crying too.

Wounds

i pricked my finger
and watched the
blood run down
red and warm
stained my clothes
spots on the ground
finger's bleeding
no sensation
just pain in my heart

tears ran down
staining my face
staining my clothes
spots on the ground
let them dry
one dries brown
one dries clear

the unseen pain lingers longer
the undetected pain hurts most

Good Morning

She softly whispered

"Good morning"

to each tear that fell down her cheeks

until the throbbing on either side of her throat

made her wish the pain

would stay in her heart.

"I cried myself to sleep last night",

she telepathically reported to the walls.

"There was no one to call. No one to listen,"

she shamefully recanted to the sheets

as she burrowed her head

under the pillows.

The Lies
the lies you tell
shatter the walls of
the kingdom of truth
crashing they fall
fall to the ground
another building
another heart
more emotions
shattered

Modern Day Pauper

Poor
hands
can't
reach
doors
with
golden
handles.

Tears Dry

tears dry by morning leaving
red puffy eyes and wet sheets.

water stains evoke
faded memories of pain
inflicted to the heart and not the skin.

you diffused into me so deep.
past the layers.
through the bone.

do you know how painful it is
to extract bone marrow?

by trying to steal you,
she almost stole my life.

can i sue the hospital for malpractice?
can i have her license taken away?

no.
he signed a directive
that gave her rights.

i am helpless.
forced to compromise.

tears dry by morning leaving
red puffy eyes and wet sheets.

Apples & Trees

i wonder at which moment we wake up
and become our mothers
folding our towels so the tags won't show
folding our underwear into three
using lines like "there's a thin line between smart and stupid"

i wonder at which moment we wake up
and become our mothers
big toe fat just like hers
weight gain in the same places she called love handles
driving too fast or driving too slow
like she did
beating conch with our hair wrapped up
wearing aprons they don't even sell anymore
then here comes her laugh up from our bellies

i wonder when we become our mothers
wearing sarongs around the house because
we're tired of clothes and society says
we can't be naked
(but secretly we want to be naked)
hanging our bras on the door for no other reason than
"i saw mummy do that"

then old family friends say
"you look just like ya ma"
and daddy says
"you act just like ya ma"
then we look in the mirror
or repeat a phrase
and realize
"i turned into my mother"
ha

In Misery I Am Yours and You Are Mine
(In Response to the 2010 Earthquake in Haiti)

naked feet are pierced
by broken glass
hard soles know pain
but feel none

bare hands grasp splintered wood
as blood stains dirty palms
leaving tracks and memories
of wounds sustained

tears chase the sorrows
that drift from blistered eyes
fall upon cracked lips
that know no other taste
and are swallowed

hearts hang loose
behind ribs as crushed
as the hopes once cherished
begging gravity to be a friend
and not a foe

who listens to the wounded organ
that has no voice
just beats?

who catches the tears that fall
on parched lips or feels the pain endured
by bodies sailing to distant lands
falling into nameless graves?

cells scream for water
water!
while it falls endlessly from weary eyes
dehydration and starvation kill
those who have survived
while i sit and watch
with eyes seldom fixated on the TV screen
that brings misery into my bedroom

with fingers moist from lifting a cold
glass of water to a moisturized mouth
and a heavy tongue
i sit and i listen
to the wounded organ in my chest
that has no voice
just beats
and hear the voice of many
because in misery
we are all one

My Little Lie

If I had to tell someone the truth
That person would have to be me
You say you want the truth
But you prefer the lie
Because I cannot hide
The pain in my eyes
Or the tears I would have to cry
If I exposed the layers of my mind
So here Mister Friend and Madam Confidant
Today I offer you
My little lie

Psalm 51

slowly walking across cold tiles
praying i don't wake up a soul
because this time i'm shunning people
i want to be alone

no jacket, no long pants
just a whole lot of skin
and a whole heap of pain
deep down within

i'm racing outside
not caring for my keys
i just need a quiet place
to get down on my knees

cry til my heart is empty
cry til my eyes are sore
Lord i need your guidance
more than ever before

don't turn your face from me
don't be like them
please give me your hands
and erase all my sin

i'm tired of chasing dreams that aren't mine
i'm tired of people pleasing
wasting all kinds of time

i'm tired of trying to do what i can't
i'm tired of crying for
things not meant to last

i keep begging for friends
who just aren't there
i keep crying these rivers
because i need you to care

forgive and forget
don't be too harsh
i've got nails in my hands
and a whole bunch of scars

set my heart on fire
dry my eyes
make my life right
so that i can try
to move forward, move upward
anywhere but here

i'm begging
i'm pleading
i'm bleeding
right here

Girl on the Bus

He hit me again. If I was light-skinned my legs would have purple bruises where he pounded his fists into my flesh. But I am dark like stained mahogany. The purple marks fade into my skin leaving only tiny ripples. There is no evidence of a love turned cold; a love that has taken on a new form of emotion and has gotten too unbridled to control. As I stand to get off of the crowded bus I feel the aches in my thighs. I stumble a little as the bus stops suddenly and sigh with immense gratitude for the railing that prevented my fall. Each step sends a painful shock up my leg forcing me to clench my jaw and ball my fists. If I was soft I would walk with a limp, but I am strong and hardened like the heels of my grandmother. Then again maybe I'm proud. Maybe I am ashamed. Sometimes some tasks become so mundane you do them without even thinking. This journey to work—two busses and a ten minute walk—is like second nature. I can lose myself within myself and allow my thoughts to fill me. I wonder how I look to people as I pass them by: consumed in my own world, unassuming, lost? A mirror could never tell me. Perhaps an unsuspecting photograph could.

The Thin Line

early in the morning
past dreams one, two and three
i heard your voice
i heard your name
i heard the plea

the "one more time"
the "i can change"
the shameless tears
it's all the same

tore down my heart
left it bare and scarred
made loving ugly
made kindness marred

took my hand
squeezed it too tight
tried to embrace me
forgot I'm shorter
more like suffocated me
because I am shorter

tears ran down
(all mine)
mental aches
(the worse kind)

walked away
more like walking to you
turned away
more like facing you

lay down on the ground
the earth is cool and moist
look at the stars
i've made my choice
i made my choice

stay and heal
the jobs not done
take the pain
say it loud
"you just lost one"

underneath skin
behind the smile
flowing between cells
that's my love for you

my love isn't stagnant
ever flowing
ever going
don't make me waste it
on a towel
or a shirt
or the ground

I Am Dust

I died a silent death and was placed in a wooden coffin. No one came to my funeral. No one saw my blood. My organs withered inside of me. My flesh did not rot—it dried and turned to dust. One day the Wind blew through the coffin and sailed me through the air. As I travelled I begged not to be returned to the Earth. I was not ready to let things grow using the ashes of my former self. Instead, I chose to settle onto faces and objects. People wiped me off with rags or coughed me back into the air. Now I no longer have choices. I can no longer choose the Earth and the green. I can only be wiped, dusted and sneezed away: a nuisance to the hands that must rid their homes of me. Troubled, I sought out answers from the skies. "What about me?" I asked of the Wind as it blew by one day. "Can I be wiped off too? Humans can't do it so what about you?" He laughed in a high-pitched whistle as he blew through a tree. I thought about what he meant then I agreed: I am dust, I can never be cleaned.

Taken

Heart wide open
Arms outstretched
"Take. Take. Take."

Who can stop you?
Who would stop you
If the sign reads "For Free"?

Souls no longer dwell within bodies
They drift outside of skeletons
So I freely offer you my flesh and bones
"Take. Take. Take."

Give nothing in return
After all isn't that the motto of a man?
My virtue is mine, mine alone
A gift given by God
Why would I waste it on you
The far-from-the-one?

There are things you may have
And things you can never take away
I make the distinction
"Take. Take. Take."

Black Bird Pie

The three of us divided a pie
that five of us had to share
because six of us had to eat.

Two of us went to sleep
with bellies full of a little less than nothing
and a little more than something.

Half of them woke us up
because they could not sleep.

So we all lay there awake
because we did not have enough to eat.

I filled myself with memories
of when the pie was just my own.

She filled herself with memories
of sweets and ice cream cones.

The others savored pieces
of a pie that was so sweet.

Still, yet still, no one had enough to eat.

Belly sore, belly sore.
The headaches are all next.

If you want to eat your fill
find a bird with an empty nest.

His Girl

when i step
i step correct
i keep him thinkin
that he's blessed
no ego trippin
neva slippin
steady keepin
women tippin
that's why they call me his girl

Running On and Out of Love

You make him your everything
and give him almost anything
but to him everything is a scary thing
so he starts sharing things
and you start giving less and less
until he sees what's been lost
but by then it's useless
because you gave your everything
to someone who was sharing things
so those people got what you had
and now what you have
isn't enough to give.

Expectations

expectations rise and fall like ocean waves
they tower high like skyscrapers
disappointment brings ground zero
the things that made you smile
now make you sigh
a skeleton of the self he knew
is what you become
void of the feelings that made you hurt
because that's what he wants
if he only knew, if he only knew
that the emotions that carried the hurt
carried the love too

Hang Me Up One Time

He hung up on me
I heard silence
Then those beeps
Those nagging beeps
Racing against my heartbeat
Winning
Stabbing me
Stomping on me
With cleats
Prepared to hurt
Prepared to destroy
Me?
Prepared to lose
Tears flow off rhythm
The beeps are fast and piercing
How pathetic
I let a phone break my heart

My Heart

Once again
I put it on the line
To let it drain.
I cried.
No, I wept.
I thought about it
Late at night
And longed for it
All day,
But it's gone.

Ladies, Stop Kissing Frogs

 I kissed a frog
 He remained a frog
 But they gave him a crown
 Because he had me
 Had me
 [wicked laugh]
 Had me
 [heavy sigh]
 Had me
 [cries]

Used To

Boy you abused my feelings
And tore my heart apart
I should have seen the signs
But you caught me off guard
I dealt with the heartache
Now I'm past that phase
If I saw you now
I wouldn't look your way
No, I'm not resentful
It's a lesson learned
Call it karma baby
It's soon gone be your turn
Yeah, you made me cry
Yeah, you had me down
But I'm strong baby
I'm sure you see that now
Cause now I've closed the door
On all that used to be
And now I use "Used to…"
To refer to
You and me

Fantasy/Fallacy

i may live in
a fantasy world.
i may live in a lie.
but at least while
i live there, no one
can make me cry.

RunDriveSwim Cowards

You won't remember the conversation
And she won't remember the revelation
You'll be in your car nodding to the vibrations
She'll be on her bed letting the pain sink in
Every three and half minutes
Your mind changes and the song switches
Your heart goes to your toes and you push down
The wind blows through your hair
And keeps your eyes dry
Drive
Drive to the other end of a small island
Drive far away from the heart that you've broken
Drive away from the pain
And go into the water
Swim
Swim good
You're free as she stains pages
And imprisons her kindness in cages
Eventually she flees from the pain
And stops herself from going insane
As her soul drives away in a Prelude

Wilting Flower

Beautiful flower with petals so bright
Wither not as the night sky falls
I beg you, wither not
But as you die, as you must do
And another bud grows ready to replace you
Let your weary petals fall into my soft hands
Let your fragile colors grace my palm
And I will bury you with a sweet, sweet song
Under the very tree you fell from

Beautiful flower your time is short
You have from dawn til dusk to leave your mark
But rest assured your bloom
Has touched the hearts of many
Tomorrow, sweet tomorrow, a new flower
Perhaps not as beautiful as you
Perhaps more stunning than you
Shall sit upon these branches
But dear, beautiful flower
Now brown and resting in rich soils
I will only think of you

It's Okay

It's okay because I have no scars
It's okay because it doesn't hurt anymore
It's okay because I no longer cry myself to sleep

It's okay because the time you kicked me, I got up
It's okay because the time you spit in my face, I washed my face
It's okay because even though I have a bump
Showing that my jaw has not realigned
I can still talk fine and I look fine
It's okay

It's alright that you cheated on me
It's alright that you fucked another girl four days before
I flew across the Atlantic to say Hi to your dick
Yeah it's alright

It's alright that you claimed she was just a friend
It's alright that you stayed up past 3AM texting
This one
That one
Her and her and her

It's alright that when I saw the BBM message
And wanted to fight you
That you fought back
It's alright that you punched me three times in my arm
To form a perfect purple circle
To get me to "calm down"

It doesn't matter that you tore off my self esteem
It doesn't matter that you made me wish I could carve out
The part of me that was white
And "of the Devil"
It doesn't matter that I would sit and look at my skin
Reaching the borderline of crazy
Wondering where white started and black ended so
I could tear out the part of me you didn't like
The part you said made me a bitch

It doesn't matter
That I had an anxiety attack in public
It doesn't matter that I cried to my dead mother
Begging her to take me because I can't do this
It does not matter that I felt alone
That the whole world was calling but I had no phone
Because you threw it in the snow

It does not matter
That I have tried to hit you and slap you
And tear you down with my words
Only to feel a blow I could never have power to give
No it doesn't matter
When you kicked me as I cried
You kicked me as I cried
You kicked me as I cried
With your strong soccer legs
When you punched me in that same leg and I screamed

It does not matter
That I sat in a counselor's chair
Trying to figure out how to kill
This
Angry
Battered
Woman
It doesn't matter that she couldn't help me
It doesn't matter that people thought I was crazy
I do not care

Although I still shed tears because
I remember how my heart was broken
I know my spirit never was
Even though I still have flashbacks
I have found a way to trust
Because I learned that God is bigger than you
I was led away from Egypt
Through the Red Sea of my tears and blood
I was delivered
And I have forgiven you

I have learned to never raise my hand
To never threaten
To answer with a gentle tongue
And not a slave master's whip
I have learned that this is life
And I have to get a grip

I have learned that it is not okay
It is not alright
It does matter
And that I do care

I have learned that to tear you down will not raise me up
I have learned that within the sheep's skin can be a wolf
I have learned that I can still love through my abuse
I have learned that I can walk away from yesterday
Because what is yesterday
Should not dictate what I say yes to today

I have learned that in my hands I hold strength
In my heart I hold will
In my mind I can hold peace
With my feet I can be firm
And with my legs I can walk away

Today it is okay
Today it is alright
Today it does not matter
Today I do not care
That I went through the valley of the shadow of death
Because today I am here
And I have learned
That I am okay

I'm okay

The Ex

Once upon a time,
on a dark night dressed in blue,
you saw the good in me
and I saw the good in you.

Smoke & Ashes

All of your problems go up in the smoke.
You watch the grey rise into the air and draw another pull.
This joint is personal.
You think about the way she makes you feel.
Ashes fall.
You think about her hands on your skin.
Smoke rises.
You tell yourself you only need THC.
Ashes fall.
You exhale and form an 'O'.
Smoke rises.
You say fuck her TLC.
Ashes fall.
Smoke rises.
Ashes fall.
Smoke rises.
You cough a little —
On the truth, not the smoke.
You think, "Maybe I missed a seed."
You take a long pull.
Your eyelids drop.
You lean your head back
And relax.
Ashes fall.
Memories fade.
Ashes fall.
Memories fade.
"You don't need her."
"She's not the one."
Memories fade.
Ashes fall.
Smoke rises.

Overstanding

They don't understand you,
but I was there for you —
always aware of you and your potential,
your thuggish ways and strong arms.
You were quick to slice with your sharp tongue
or pound with your quick fists
to prove to someone, anyone,
that you were bad-man heterosexual.
I saw you deep inside
and watched the sun rise in your eyes
and oceans quake with your every breathe.
Misunderstood, yet so easy to overstand.

Diary of A Teenager - Part 1

You're a page I tore out. I didn't realize I pressed so hard that the words had printed onto other pages. If I tear the others out the whole book will fall apart. You're a page I tore out. A chapter I wanted to be over. Embarrassing pages stained by my tears. Oh the amount of times I cried over you. The amount of times I ripped the page with my pen because my feelings irritated me. Why did I like you so much? I couldn't understand this was my first glimpse at love. Unrequited. Unreturned. Wasted. On someone who didn't care. Someone who couldn't see that one day I would be beautiful. Someone who didn't want to bear the guilt of hurting me. (Although all the times you ignored me hurt me.) Now that I have more power I throw fits for being ignored. You're a page I tore out. As I look closely at the other pages I see all those words I wrote about you. All I wanted was you. So childish. So naive. I convinced myself you were perfect for me. I loved your walk and the way you dressed. Every time I saw you I was reminded of island breezes. You? Cool, collected and smiling. You'd flash me a wicked grin and have questions and taunting in your eyes. I wonder if you ever felt what I did. I remember you missing me when I trained myself not to call. I remember that once. I remember you liked me a little bit, but never enough to make me more than just a friend. I was just a friend. I turned the smallest things you did into bigger things, meaningful things. I ignored the signs of lack of interest. In a way I should respect that you wanted to save me from you and you the player. In a way I should respect that you knew you weren't mature enough to be with just me so you sent me out into the world holding on to that beautiful memory of my first love. Then too I can be mad. Enraged even. Because you sent me out into a cruel world to be hurt by this one, betrayed by that one and played by him, then him, then him. Honestly I would have preferred it be you. You made me smile without trying. Being around you was so easy. I piled up the tiny moments and I had a book of memories that I crammed into this book. You're a page I tore out. A page I threw away. Many days ago from yesterday and here you are. Crumpled yes, but here. I want you no less than those ten years ago when I was a very different little girl. I still hold on to memories of you and wish I had more and more and more. You're a reason to write a new book. A reason to no longer be embarrassed of my feelings because that's how you make me feel. That's how you always make me feel. A little stupid. A little stupid to believe that you could see my worth now and make an effort now. A little stupid to lay myself bare and pray you accept me and claim me the way I had pictured long ago. A little stupid, I admit, to think you were ready at not-so-young-as-then-but-still-too-young-right-now to truly appreciate that I'm here and won't be here for long. Again you send me out to be hurt by this world. This time. This final time. I'll come back with a ring and many things not to make you jealous, but to show you that I have lived. And lived a wonderful life. The life in my belly is beautiful with eyes like mine that shine and love and give. My husband hugs me every day and calls me amazing because at times I kinda am. He's not you. Not my first love. But he's my last love. The love that took the time to wait on me to realize it was pointless waiting on you. He's the one who calls me his first love. He's the one I ignored. He's the one I made just a friend. He's the one I would push aside as I lived life too afraid to commit to anyone but you. He's the one. And I can't say I wish he was you because it wouldn't be fair to him if that were true.

Strange Snowmen
(For Kags)

i felt the snow beneath my toes
the chill of ice
the frostbitten nose
i felt my tears
crack on my face
and large warm hands
steal an embrace
i felt him lift me from the street
he force-fed me
the same two words he'd repeat
"Calm down."
"Calm down."

i heard them sing me off to sleep
each beautiful word
i tried to keep
but my eyes were heavy
from the pain inside
my feet were hurting
i think i cried
the water burned my cold, red face
i screamed and screamed
for an escape
i tore my clothes and felt bare skin
i saw them look at me like i was sin

pain is ugly
pain is heavy
pain tattooed on my belly
pain in my heart
pain in my eyes
pain at the parting of my thighs
i think i cried

the water burned my cold, red face
i screamed and screamed
for an escape
i tore my clothes
and bore my skin
they walked away
for i have sinned

Vain Attempts

Busy whirlwinds
Cloud the mind
Causing
Bewilderment
Temporary insanity
Confusion
Time spills away
Hear it as it leaks from your veins
It cannot be stopped
Its speed cannot be altered
Why try?

Yup, I'm a Woman

I've always been told there's a thin line between being smart and being stupid—likewise with love and hate. That said, I'm walking on thin lines trying to keep my balance in these five inch heels. Secretly, I'm gritting my teeth because beauty (and wisdom) always come with pain. Yup, I'm a woman or steadily growing into one. Advised to look before plunging, analyze before stepping and think before speaking. Submission at all four corners of the square. Stop signs at all angles in the 360 degree sphere termed this world. Yup, I'm a woman or trying to live up to the image of one. Bold, brave and adventurous in perfectly measured quantities so I don't upset the ego of a man. Elegant, polite, beautiful, classy, and intelligent to fit into stereotypes. Bare foot, natural and full of a dialect I wouldn't let go for my mother because I let freedom reign (in spite of the consequences). I wear my flaws on my face, my heart on my sleeve, my pain in my eyes and love all over every square inch of me because I am a woman and ashamed is something that I'll never be.

Big Belly Girl

Belly big wit child da doctor neva see
Feet swell, chin gone
She heavy down wit pickney
Whispers on da street "Her ma n pa…" dis dat
Say dey disappointed she big up by some riff raff
U know dis girl, dis here girl, u talkin roun town bout?
U know her mind?
U know her style?
So why u run ya mouth?
Can't be u Miss Ting who Grammy had six babies
Unwed to dis day
Can't be u Mista Man
Who impregnate tree[1] bus-ridin girls same year
Enn u hey?
Den u wan come open up ya yellow teet
Talkin to da neighbours bout da neighours til errybody weak
She workin hard to mek a way fa her baby wit no shame
She have a good man who ga be dere willin and proud to claim
But une don't care dat she graduate wit honours
Or that she bin thru trial and trial and made it through dem horrors
U just pile tings on da list to make ya gossip sweeter
Den when someone come to ya porch ya'll talk n talk til ya see her
U don't care bout her character and dat she got sound mind
Neda da plans she made or money she saved workin overtime
All u see is big belly, sinful girl who makin and made a mistake
She see life, she see hope cause dis here girl got faith
Yes da two gone struggle
Yeah it gone be hard
But don't u doubt dis big belly girl
Cause her dreams can't be fenced in like ya lil back yard
Belly swell, feet sore yet glowin all da while
Cause while ya face all sour up she proud to carry her child

[1]three

Wise Men Are Proactive

He said she was too cool—too girl next door—because she preferred baggy pants and Converse or even going bare foot. He said she hardly fixes her hair and doesn't like make-up so he couldn't stunt with her. He couldn't flaunt with her. He said she hid her sex appeal so no one would be jealous. Be jealous. Be jealous. Now he has a girl who dresses up every day. She wears the make-up, the lashes, and the heels. Her hair is always on point (even if she has to buy it). Still, sometimes he looks at her and realizes that she's not pretty. Or maybe she is pretty, but something's missing. She's just not beautiful. He thinks to himself: "Her eyes don't shine just for me. She puckers her lips to take pictures so you never see her true smile. She flaunts so much that there's nothing left for us to share alone. She has to put on a face to get a face that commands attention. I wish I had my ex who turned heads without trying. She dressed on those rare occasions and commanded her section of the room. She was beautiful and it showed even on the days we were just kicking it. She was beautiful. Maybe I should have told her more. Maybe I should have kept her."

Eleuthera

isle of rich red soils
bleeding into pineapples
yellow and sweet
call me home

land of limestone cliffs
stand high and proud
for me to see
across the waters
that separate us
call me home

frothy waves
kiss the shores
i have slept on
erase the footprints
that are not mine
claim your territory once more
and give me space
to plant my feet
in soft pink sands
untrodden
by shoe nor toe
bring shells and sea fans
to my grasp
to increase my collection
call me home

wait sunsets
that kiss coconut leaves goodnight
wait moonlight
that glistens over still waters
wait wind
that whistles through the bushes i played in
wait sunrise
that kisses the buds of annual crops

wait rains
that moisturize my paths
wait sea grapes
that stain my tongue with violet sweetness
wait pigeon plums, coco plums, mangoes
and all that I love
wait for me one more night
may your roads claim no more friends
may your rage claim no more family members
call me home

Lukku-Cairi

Red skinned Lucayans hidden in thick brush and limestone caves
Send heartfelt cries to Taino ears high on mountain peaks
Scratches leak blood of the same consistency of Caribs
Whose scars glisten in the sun as they fight back
With poisoned arrows, sharpened stones and piercing bones
Once separated from Tainos
By years of vile war, savageness and cannibalism
United now in a front to save
Their beautiful land of water and green
From pale faces who only see
In shades of green, gold and white pearl
Fragile minds enslaved and afraid
As they mourn the lynched Caciques
That hang from the branches of mango trees
Quinep trees, sycamore trees, silk cotton trees
Or fall broken and rotten to the ground
To be savored by Spanish dogs
Mange, rabies, fleas
New born babies torn in half at the limbs
As blood splatters over the faces of heartbroken mothers
With breasts still warm and leaking
Ravenous dogs devour the bodies that mount high
Trying to touch a blue sky that now has a glass ceiling
To the South they pray
To the Sun they pray
To ancestors who lived long ago
To ancestors murdered yesterday
To the zemis in their huts smelling of cassava and maize
To the zemis around their necks made of bone, stone and wood
They pray
To be swallowed whole by sharks as they dive
To die with dignity from starvation and dehydration
To have the courage to take their own lives
And the lives of their children
Before one more day is spent at the hands of the Spanish
With their horses, gun powder, dogs, Bibles, swords and evil
With a weapon of mass destruction so dark
And hardened by brutality: a black heart

Blood has no time to dry before they kill again
At the mere hesitation to follow an order
From lack of comprehension
Of a strange tongue and hate-filled eyes
Again their blood stains the rocks I walked upon as a child
Their whispers float in the cool breeze that hits my face
As I watch the sun set in orange, pink, purple, red, and deep blue
I climb trees deep in the bush
And look over at the land they fought to keep
I stand barefoot on the soil so red I swore to my mother
It was their blood crying out like Abel from the slaughter
The inhabitants of my land centuries before my birth
I bare a name that unites me to them forever
I dig my feet deep into the soil and pray
They know that I remember their struggle
I plant fruit trees, my favorite delicacies, and travel with the roots
To kiss their bones Good Night and Good Morning

My people

Assurance

Today I went to the beach alone
I sat in the ocean, looked up at the sky
And asked God,
"Are you okay?"
Suddenly the sun came out from behind a cloud
The rays tiptoed across the waves
Until they touched my outstretched hand
I smiled and asked of Him,
"So does that mean you're fine?"
My eyes darted from cloud to cloud
Looking for what might be an answer
To my right, nestled between two rainclouds,
Was a cloud rainbow
The colors danced, suspended in the sky
I smiled again—
God's fine

Nut Shell

turned inside out
and upside down
incomprehensible
to the lazy
and out of bounds
to the stupid
mind dances
carefully anticipating
the flash of lashes
hidden behind the smile
the eyes
and the scars
far, far away
from reality
that's me

Cinnamon Scented Day Dream

I saw him in a dream I had as I lay awake on the sofa wishing for things that weren't mine to claim. I heard his voice ringing in my ear and felt his warm breath on my cheek as he leaned in to whisper to me. To my sensory system his breath smelt like cinnamon, sweet cinnamon. It took me a moment to take him in. My eyes rolled back to places I know they can't reach, and I exhaled. I spoke of him to people who wouldn't remember his name — just the sound of my voice as the syllables escaped my lips. I watched his hands grip hold of mine and felt the strength of a love I wish I could tie down and marry. All in my dreams, my wonderful day dreams; the ones I wish I stole from reality and helped fate to craft.

Deloniz Regia: The Flame Tree

Under the Poinciana tree I dreamed a million dreams and carefully whispered them to the buds so that they could bloom and blaze like fire. Out of the dry shrubs stood an explosion of red and, sometimes, sun-kissed yellow. I smile at the wonder of a tree that seems so bare and boney during most of the year. Its summertime leaves so green shade my eyes from the harsh sun that wishes to turn me crimson. The flaming orange and red petals decorate the ground and give the ants new things to carry (although I don't understand why they would). As a child, a Poinciana tree could entertain for hours. We tore apart the unopened buds and stuck them on our fingers as nails. We played games with the stamen to see who could keep their anther the longest. We picked the petals off one by one to see which classmate was destined to be our one true love. We painted faces on the seed casings or opened them up to use the seeds as decoration for our crafts. We climbed the fragile branches and hung upside down in the breeze or chased each other with the soft leaves. Now I lay on a carpet of flaming petals shaded by a million tiny leaves whispering heart-felt prayers and my deepest dreams.

Just A Wish

i want to

brighten up your life
and make you smile
like a cool
summer's day

i want to

catch your eye
like a lone flamingo
in a mangrove swamp

i want to

capture you
with my dark eyes
and cradle you
under my wings

we may not fly far
but we can fly away

Pillow Talk

When the pillow is soft
and the room is dark
eyes can close
and heads can rest
upon the softness of cotton
in the darkness of night.

Family Reunion

She lives in Eleuthera
and gently holds Donovan's hand
as they sit on Co's cliffs.
Together they watch the water glisten.
Their eyes shine with happiness
while they watch the sun climb up the sky
and fall back into the sea.
The winds blow them to my roof top
and I spend my mornings with them.
Tears fall and veil my smile.

Please Visit the Garden
(For Grandma Audrey)

The flowers of your garden are swaying in the breeze
Eager to feel your hands against their leaves
The butterflies are dancing and watching for your gaze
Although your hands no longer tilled the soil
The buds knew your voice
The fritillaries knew the curve of your smile
And the joyfulness of your laugh as you watched them play
Now the painted lady is missing her tea partner
The buddleia is swaying lower now
She misses her old friend
Will you promise to visit with the wind every now and again?
Will you promise to gently touch the leaves
While nestled in a raindrop?
As the single drop slides down the buds will smile
Because their dear friend is never further
Than a spring shower away
They'll look for you in the morning dew
And await you with the summer breeze
Please visit often to this place where butterflies dance for you
Where bees await the sweet drinks placed on your table
And sweet fragrances from beautiful flowers engulf every visitor
Please visit often Audrey
Until then, your garden will miss you

Spring Time, Growth Time

i was a bud waiting
on just another month to be a rose
then the frost came early
so early that my eyes never saw the sun
and my sweet aroma did not attract a single bee
i turned brown and withered away
my life i stored within the stem
this year i shall bloom
spring says
grow again

Now
My heart is big, not broken.
My faith is firm, not shaken.
My smile is bright, not faded.
My self is true, not jaded

Made in the USA
Charleston, SC
31 January 2015